Contents:

My Name Is Ray and I'm an addict

It's An Epidemic

Is It Really Harmful?

Are You Hooked? The Real Issue

Myths About Porn

What Does the Bible Say? Steps To Freedom

    1. Turn To Jesus!
    2. Spend Time With God Daily
    3. Choose Your Allies
    4. Count The Consequences
    5. Identify Your Triggers
    6. "HALT"
    7. Dig Out The Roots
    8. Take Authority Over Your Eyes
    9. Grow In God's Word
    10. Pray Continually
    11. Get Involved
    12. The Anointing breaks the yoke

Pray this Prayer

Is Masturbation Sin?

Further Reading & Resources

Preface

My Name Is Ray and I'm an Addict

At the age of 10 I was introduced to pornography through a magazine one of my friends bought to school. From this my appetite began to increase -I wanted to see more. After this initial introduction I was at a friend's house and it was at that very moment for the first time in my life I saw an X- RATED movie, immediately I was hooked. Wherever I could go and have a look I would, from page 3 girls to X rated movies. At the age of 16 I started to secretly purchase penthouse and forum magazines. At one point in time I even solicited a prostitute, I wanted and needed more. I was in church functioning in my church office with no remorse no feeling. Once I got into marriage I thought it would stop, however after many years it came back with a vengeance (seven more demons worse than before). I started buying videos and attending X-rated movie theatres. I was out of control... I was married, I was in ministry but none of those was as powerful as the pornography. The birth of the internet added intrigue and easier accessibility to my addiction. I no longer had to pay for just a few clicks and there it was I was hooked.

I couldn't tell anyone because everything I had worked towards and loved would have been taken away. I was sick but had no doctor. I was leading a double life, one I could control and the other was controlling me.

One day in the heat of depression, guilt and shame I cried out to God from the pits of disappear. I realize that my life was unmanageable and I had lost control. I went to a pastoral friend and shared with him my state of mind. Praise God he was clued up on spiritual warfare, He and his elders performed an exorcism and after prayer and anointing a few hours later I felt liberated and lifted in Jesus.

This then led me to attend a Christian 12 step Group. The first session I walked out on because I had felt like I didn't want to be there. But something kept pushing me to come back. The second time I stayed and even shared my testimony. I felt safer there than at church. Nobody was there to cast judgments or have an opinion because everyone in that room admitted that they too needed help.

It was in those meetings that they told me that My healing was being dependent on my high power (God) and telling my story to help other addicts to be set free. Ever since that day I have not been ashamed of my past and I am a better person today because of what I have been through.

I'm not telling you that overnight I magically got healed, I still get weak from time to time (when I take my eye of God) I have slipped and made mistakes, But I repent Quickly, I claim the blood of Jesus and only through deliverance and trust in Him is why I'm in a better place today.

This book is my attempt to share some of the tools that has helped me in my Journey to this point. I pray it will help you. Please feel free to contact me if you need someone to talk to and pray with. God loves you and he always will.

God wants us to walk in the power of the Holy Spirit and to experience His victory in every area of our lives.

Tragically, sin and addiction can quickly rob us of the joy and freedom we should enjoy through Christ Jesus.

Sin has been around since Satan convinced Adam and Eve that they needed something outside of God's will. By them doing so you can see the effects in our culture today. Behavior that used to be considered shameful is now flaunted. Recently, there has been an astronomical rise in the amount of pornography, which is readily available over the Internet, on television, and in other media. Consequently, more people are exposed to it – and more are hooked. Although Christians may think they should be immune to pornography's attraction, increasing numbers of believers are falling prey to its powerful lure and becoming addicted.

If you feel trapped in an endless cycle of lust, guilt, and broken promises, God wants to set you free! Jesus said, "The thief comes only to steal, and kill, and destroy; I have come that they may have life, and might have it abundantly" (John 10:10, NRSV). The Bible promises that the power of sin is broken by Christ as we surrender to Him (see Romans 6:1-14).

As you read these words, may you discover how much God wants to forgive you, deliver you, and give you the abundant life that He has promised to all who follow Him.

This is my time to share with you and tell you that no matter how far you think you have gotten from grace, the ultimate grace giver is waiting for you. Today with my head held high I profess and proclaim:

My name is Ray, I'm an addict saved only by His grace.

Thousands messages come to me from men and women of all walks of life who struggle with addictions to pornography, masturbation, cybersex, and similar sexual practices (they must of heard of my struggles). We have seen many lives and families devastated by addictive sexual sins. These problems are not unique to any race, financial, social or marital status—Christian or non-Christian. If you suspect that you may have such an addiction, or you know someone who has, this book is for you.

It's An Epidemic

A Christian may think he or she is the only believer in town struggling with porn. Unfortunately, that's far from true. Addiction to pornography is rapidly becoming an epidemic throughout our society and even in the Church.

Every second - $3,075.64 is being spent on pornography **Every second** - 28,258 Internet users are viewing pornography
Every second - 372 Internet users are typing adult search terms into search engines

Every 39 minutes a new pornographic video is being created in the United States, in Canada. Statistically, every person spends $30.21 in purchasing pornography per year.
Of those who view pornography on a regular basis, 75% are men, 25% are women. Statistics state that 40 million adults access porn sites on a regular basis.

Now the shocking statistics

90% of youth have seen pornography via Internet, movie or magazine before they are 16 years of age, the average age of exposure to porn being just 11 years of old.

It's not just youth accessing porn, Christian men were surveyed at a Christian convention. 53% admitted to viewing pornography in the week before the convention. 47% of Christians in NA will admit that pornography is a problem in their home.

Very few, if any of us are untouched by this dynamic. Our televisions give us half hour sitcoms with dozens of comments containing sexual innuendo. Advertising specializes in skin exposure. I need not go on. The point is simple, we live in a culture where sex sells, where the desire for profit knows that sex sells, where there is very little sense of shame and modesty, where the cultural air we breathe is sexualized. And if you have struggled with pornography, you know its power to consume your soul, gut your relationship with God, defeat your Christian witness and make you feel like hell is a present reality.

The main reason for those feelings are simple, what used to be available only in a city's red-light district is now in plain view on the covers of sexy magazines at convenience stores ... in Hollywood films, TV shows and commercials ... on life- size posters at the mall and larger-than-life billboards along the highway ... in suggestive lingerie ads in the Sunday newspaper ... and on millions of web sites.

Years ago, people had to take a risk to visit an "adult bookstore" – after all, they might be seen by someone they knew! But with the Internet, people can now inflame and indulge their sexual appetites with erotic material at any time, in any neighborhood, in the total privacy of their living rooms.

Although pornography is more common among men, many women are also becoming hooked – not so much by visual imagery, but by the emotional intimacy available through Internet chat rooms.

People often hope that their desire for porn will diminish when they get married or grow older, but the emotional and physiological factors can be continuing problems.

Is It Really Harmful?

Many people deny or rationalize their use of porn, saying: "It's only entertainment! What's the harm in looking at pictures? God created beautiful bodies, and I enjoy seeing them. After all, looking doesn't hurt anybody!"

The truth is, looking at pornographic images erodes healthy relationships and can easily become a pathway to adultery and other serious problems. Sexual intercourse within marriage draws a couple together physically, emotionally and spiritually, as they desire to please one another; and if a couple chooses it can bring forth and produce the gift of children. In contrast, self-stimulation and sexual gratification for its own sake is simply to fulfill one's own lust.

Men who ogle photos of idealized, airbrushed glamour girls in sexy positions probably will not find satisfaction with their real-life wives. A woman who discovers her husband using porn feels betrayed. Even if he has been physically faithful to her, it's terribly hurtful to realize that he has been having emotional affairs with other women. Conversely, a man would feel betrayed to discover his wife having sexually explicit conversations with other men on the Internet.

Adolescent girls and young women are also negatively influenced by our culture's overemphasis on sexy, "perfect" bodies. Many struggle with anorexia or bulimia – or even desire plastic surgery – so they can emulate an unrealistic, "ideal" female figure.

Another side effect of the porn epidemic is evident in the workplace, where growing numbers of employees use their computers for porn – essentially stealing time and productivity from their employers. Some are so hooked that they continue looking at porn on company time even after being warned that this will result in losing their jobs.

Tragically, a casual interest in so-called "soft-core" porn can develop into an insatiable thirst for hard-core porn, leading some addicts into strip clubs, massage parlors, voyeurism, child pornography, and pedophilia.

Some people feel so hopelessly trapped that they think there is no way out. One man said that he almost committed suicide because of his lifelong addiction to pornography. He said, "I was flawed to the point where there was nothing that could be done about me. And so the only alternative was to end my life." Fortunately, he realized he was wrong – and that there is hope.

Respected counselors who work with child molesters, voyeurs, sadomasochists, and rapists say that pornography is usually a significant factor in these behaviors. Shortly before his execution, serial killer Ted Bundy invited Dr. James Dobson of Focus on the Family to interview him on death row. Bundy urgently wanted to warn people about the terrible dangers of porn.

"I was a normal person," Bundy said. "I had good friends. I led a normal life, except for this one, small but very potent and destructive segment that I kept very secret and close to myself." And so an addicting behavior that began at age 13 when he found dirty magazines in a dumpster culminated in the brutal murders of 28 innocent women and girls.

While Ted Bundy represents the extreme, "Jeff" is more typical. He and his lovely wife live in a nice suburban home with their kids and are active at church. But Jeff never felt accepted by his father and used porn to soothe the hurt. This eventually led to squandering money on prostitutes. When his wife discovered his infidelity, she was shocked to learn that they were heavily in debt, his job could be in jeopardy, and he needed to be tested for sexually transmitted diseases, including AIDS. After intensive work and Christian counseling, Jeff was delivered from his addicting actions and their marriage was saved – but even so, it was a long time before Jeff regained his wife's trust.

Yes, porn has a price – and it can cost you everything.

I'm I Hooked?

It's important to understand that sexual addictions don't happen overnight. It takes time to develop. But when they're full-blown, a man won't be able to resist the repeated urge to enter into a love relationship with a sexual object or experience that gives pleasure and the illusion of intimacy.

That last sentence defines an addict: . He's hooked and can't say no.

. The object of his addiction gives him two things: pleasure and an illusion of intimacy.

Not everyone who struggles with sexual compulsions is an addict. Some men abuse their sexuality for a period of time and then grow out of it. Many men with a regrettable sexual experience in the past put it behind them and move on.

But not everyone is so fortunate. Some men block emotional pain with sexual pleasure. Over time they have to try increasingly risky forms of sexual behavior in order to deaden the pain. Eventually their world revolves around sex. Their obsession has taken over their life.

Sexual Addiction Test (4 questions)

Patrick Carnes ask four questions aimed at helping us discover if we have a sexual addiction. While asking yourself these questions, it's crucial that you are brutally honest. The first step in dealing with a problem is admitting we have one.

Is Your Behavior Secret?

Are you doing things you refuse to tell others about? Do you feel that if those closest to you knew what you were doing, they would reject you or strongly disapprove of your actions? Are you telling lies to cover your behavior? If so, you're isolating yourself from those you love and entering into a potentially addictive relationship with an object or event.

Is Your Behavior Abusive?

Does your sexual behavior create pain (emotional, Financial or physical) for you or others? Is it degrading or exploitative of you or others? Do you find yourself

performing increasingly abusive acts?
Do you derive pleasure from watching
others being abused in some way?

Is Your Behavior Used to Numb Painful Feelings?

Are your sexual actions an effort to change your mood rather than express affections? Do you masturbate or search for some other sexual outlet when you're depressed, bored, or angry? If your sexual behavior is used to erase pain, it's part of an addictive process.

Is Your Behavior Empty of Genuine Commitment and Caring?

Are you substituting the illusion of intimacy provided by an object or event for the genuine intimacy found in a healthy relationship?

If you answered yes to even one of the four questions, your sexual behavior is either compulsive or addictive.

5 Stages of Addictions

While these four questions help determine if we have a problem, they don't tell us how bad it is. In order to determine that, we need to familiarize ourselves with the levels of addictions.

Pre-addiction

Pre-addiction describes people who begin to find themselves sexually stimulated through impersonal objects, like pornographic (topless newspapers), lusting (looking) or events, like strip clubs.

If you're at this level, your life is probably under control. You're holding down a job, and your relationship with your wife or girlfriend is intact. However, you realize that while your fascination with pornography, strip shows, or erotic talk lines isn't compulsive, it is dangerous. You may be troubled by the feeling that your slumbering lust could awaken and take over at any moment.

Stage 1

At level 1 a Person's lust has begun to exert its control. They're compulsively involved in such things as masturbation, pornography, homosexuality, or demeaning heterosexual relationships.

When a person reaches level 1, something significant has happened. While before he always struggled to keep his lust under control, now it's running wild. In his book The Addictive Personality, Craig Nakken notes that the single most important aspect of level 1 addictions is the emergence of the addictive personality.[3] Lust, like a great dragon, has awakened from its slumber and threatens to take over his life.

It's like the first time you get high on marijuana. You enter a new world and want to return to that world. There's something about that first high that people want to recreate. Similarly, a person who enters level 1 awakens their lust in a powerful way. And that initial experience is one they wants to recreate. When we enter level 1, the addictive part of our personality has been stirred. **Make no mistake about it, the beast has an insatiable appetite that can slowly take over our life.**

Stage 2

When a person reaches level 2, they've taken a bigger and more dangerous step. Now his behavior may involves victims and violations of the law. His activities can include prostitution, exhibitionism, voyeurism, obscene phone calls, and touching a person intimately without consent. Most of the time he's considered more of a nuisance than a criminal, but unfortunately his behavior can inflict deep emotional pain on his self and victims victims.

People who are exhibitionists (showing) or voyeurs (watching) will carry out their secret behavior for years. Living double lives, they're in constant fear of being caught.

All kinds of "good" people reach level 2. Hardly a week passes without a news story about a Pastor, politician, teacher, or Hollywood star picking up a prostitute or making an unwanted sexual advance etc.

Stage 3

By the time we reach level 3, his behavior involves serious crimes in which severe damage is done to the victim. Rape, incest, child molestation, loss of family and self respect occur at this level.

Stages 4

When you get to level 4, Get ready for destruction.

By now you should know if you're hooked. You should also have a feel for how far your sexual compulsion has progressed. While most of us would prefer avoiding the truth for as long as we can, eventually the moment of truth will arrive. Something will happen to force you to admit that your life is out of control.

- You'll accidentally leave a pornographic image on your computer monitor, and someone at work will report it to your boss.
- One of your kids will find your stash of X-rated videos.
- A policeman will arrive at your place of work because a neighbor has identified you as a Peeping Tom.
- Your wife will leave because you've had another affair.
- The school counselor will call because you've been reported to the child care agency for improperly touching a neighbor child.

All Is Not Lost

For Samson, the moment of truth arrived near the end of his life. Blinded by lust, he slept in Delilah's lap while a Philistine barber cut his hair. A moment after the last strand fell, his enemies burst into his presence. Isolated from God, he was powerless to resist. Israel's champion

became a bald-headed clown who entertained the Philistines.

Samson had fallen. He would never gaze at another Philistine woman. His enemies had made sure of that when they gouged out his eyes (Judges 16:20-21).

Many people believe that Samson's story ends on a tragic note. I don't. Although he was blind and imprisoned, his hair began to grow, and so did his relationship with God. The Lord forgave Samson and used him one last time. The hero of Judah pulled down a Philistine temple, destroying himself and his enemies.

Samson learned firsthand what every man must know. God is the God of a

second and third and fourth chance.
He never gives up on us

The Real Issues

Within each person, God has placed a fundamental need for intimacy. We see this clearly in creation, when God said, "It is not good for the man to be alone" (Genesis 2:18). This desire for emotional intimacy is normally filled through healthy relationships with one's parents, siblings, friends, and spouse. For various reasons, however, some people struggle to connect with others and have difficulty developing close relationships. When people feel empty on the inside, this emotional vacuum can be easily filled with a counterfeit intimacy – selfish sexual gratification. True intimacy satisfies this God-given need, but fantasies and masturbation leave people feeling empty, worthless, and trapped in a vicious cycle. The more they use pornography, the more it separates them from others and hinders their ability to develop healthy relationships. The more alone they feel, the greater their desire for intimacy, and the more they are driven to fill the void with pornography. Freedom comes by dealing with the heart – the deepest inner-core of our being.

Jesus emphasized the importance of the inner life by saying, "For from within, out of men's hearts, come evil thoughts, sexual immorality, ... [and] adultery" (Mark 7:21). Also, Paul wrote: "You must no longer live as the Gentiles do, in the futility of their thinking. They are darkened in their understanding and separated from the life of God because of the ignorance that is in them due to the hardening of their hearts. Having lost all sensitivity, they have given themselves over to sensuality so as to indulge in every kind of impurity, with a continual lust for more" (Ephesians 4:17b-19).

Myths

Here are some of the common myths about porn use…and the reality they try to hide.
Myth: Using porn is common, and that makes it okay.

Fact: Pornography use is common. It's estimated that 1 in 8 Internet searches are for erotic content.

However, this does not make it morally okay. As William Struthers explains in his book Wired for Intimacy, "Just because something is a cultural norm does not make it morally right or wrong, good or evil." In fact, our society deliberately values women for more than just reproductive capabilities. Pornography, however, leads to the objectification of women as sexual objects, which actually makes it culturally reprehensible.

Myth: There's no difference between pornography and art.

Fact: The motives behind artists and pornographers are almost always different. In art, men and women are portrayed as people, whereas in pornography, they are objects for lust. Struthers explains, "Pornography degrades and dehumanizes. Art celebrates the meaning and value of sexual intimacy between two individuals."

Myth: Pornography helps spice up your sex life.

Fact: Porn actually decreases sexual satisfaction. Porn and masturbation enable people to gratify themselves, instead of finding fulfilment with another person. Porn makes reality extremely boring.

Eventually, many men get to the point where they can no longer perform without imagining themselves in a pornographic situation. Dr. Judith Reisman explains, "If [a man] can't make love to his beloved, if he has to imagine a scene in order to actually achieve the heights of completion with this person, then he's no longer with his own power, is he? He has been stripped, he has been hijacked, he has been emasculated, he has in effect been hijacked by the *Internet, Playboy* or *Penthouse* or any of the materials that followed."

Myth: Watching porn isn't the same as cheating.

Fact: Pornography enables people to find physical satisfaction outside their married relationships.Dr. Phil says, "It is an insult, it is disloyal, and it is cheating." Ella Hutchinson, a Licensed Professional Counsellor, adds, "He is receiving sexual gratification from other women. In my mind, that is infidelity," and before marriage if fornication.

Myth for Wives: It's your fault he watches porn.

Fact: Often men have the tendency to blame-shift, claiming that if you were prettier or thinner or more open to sex or less of a nag, that they wouldn't need to turn to the fantasy that pornography provides. Even if men don't say these things, their wives will often wonder such things about themselves. Often wives will tie their own self-worth to their husbands' opinions of them. In *Partners: Healing from His Addiction,* Dr. Doug Weiss explains that a drop in self-esteem is common after a betrayal.

If your husband is telling you such things, he is trying to rationalize and justify his desire for porn by shifting the blame to you. By blaming you, he protects himself from shame and avoids any suggestion he is not adequate. If he is not ready to take responsibility for his own behaviour, "he will say anything to convince you, and even himself, that he does not have a problem. Blaming you is an easy way to save face," explains Hutchinson.

You could be the most beautiful, supportive woman in the world and he'd still turn to porn. It was there before marriage and will be there after...

What Does The Bible Say

Although God's Word doesn't specifically mention pornography, it most definitely addresses the issues of inappropriate sexual arousal and promiscuousness. The Ten Commandments say, "You shall not commit adultery" and "You shall not covet ... your neighbor's wife" (Exodus 20:14, 17). But Jesus set an even higher standard – clearly warning about the destructiveness of "just looking." He said, "You have heard that it was said, 'Do not commit adultery.' But I tell you that anyone who looks at a woman lustfully has already committed adultery with her in his heart. If your right eye causes you to sin, gouge it out and throw it away. It is better for you to lose one part of your body than for your whole body to be thrown into hell" (Matthew 5:27- 29). Jesus was using a figure of speech to say that we should take drastic action – to do whatever it takes – to stop sinning. Obviously, that means not looking with a lustful eye.

Similarly, Proverbs cautions us not to underestimate the tremendous power of visual enticement. "Do not lust in your heart after her beauty or let her captivate you with her eyes, for ... the adulteress preys upon your very life. Can a man scoop fire into his lap without his clothes being burned?" (Proverbs 6:25-27).

Also, 1 Corinthians 6:13b-15 tell us: "The body is not meant for sexual immorality, but for the Lord, and the Lord for the body. By His power God raised the Lord from the dead, and He will raise us also. Do you not know that your bodies are members of Christ Himself? Shall I then take the members of Christ and unite them with a prostitute? Never!"

The passage continues with a very interesting directive. God's Word often commands us to "stand firm" in battle. But when it comes to sexual temptation, the Bible says to run away – fast! "Flee from sexual immorality. All other sins a man commits are outside his body, but he who sins sexually sins against his own body. Do you not know that your body is a temple of the Holy Spirit, who is in you, whom you have received from God? You are not your own; you were bought at a price. Therefore honor God with your body" (vs. 18-20).

God wants us to live up to a higher standard than the world, with Jesus as our role model. We are not to live like people in the world, nor should we try to get away with as much as we can without actually breaking His laws. The world says, "What's wrong with Playboy?" But Hebrews 13:4 says, "Marriage should be honored by all, and the marriage bed kept pure, for God will judge the adulterer and all the sexually immoral." A marriage bed cannot be pure if one of the partners is fantasizing about another person. And whether we are single or married, the Bible exhorts us, "But among you there must not be even a hint of sexual immorality, or of any kind of impurity, or of greed, because these are improper for God's holy people" (Ephesians 5:3).

Galatians 5 lists many pitfalls, beginning with sexual immorality, impurity and debauchery. It concludes by giving us a clear choice: "Those who live like this will not inherit the kingdom of God. But the fruit of the Spirit is love, joy, peace, patience, kindness, goodness, faithfulness, gentleness, and self-control. ... Those who belong to Christ Jesus have crucified the sinful nature with its passions and desires.

Since we live by the Spirit, let us keep in step with the Spirit" (vs. 21b-25).

Are you ready to choose God's pathway to spiritual victory?

Steps To Freedom In Christ

Once you make a decision to turn away from sin, there are a number of important things you must do to achieve lasting triumph over temptation and addicting actions.

Turn To Jesus!

People struggling with sin may think, "I'll turn to God after I clean up my act, but I'm not good enough to come to Him yet." Here's the plain truth: you can never clean yourself up enough for God – but He will do it for you! Ephesians 2:8-9 tells us, "For it is by grace you have been saved, through faith – and this not from yourselves, it is the gift of God – not by works, so that no one can boast." Jesus loves you and paid for every single one of your sins by His death on the cross.

When you truly repent of your sins and give God your whole life – broken and messy as it may be – He gladly accepts you as His child and gives you a new life. The Bible says, "Put off your old self, which is being corrupted by its deceitful desires; to be made new in the attitude of your minds; and to put on the new self, created to be like God in true righteousness and holiness" (Ephesians 4:22-24).

This describes a new life in God! You take off the old self and are made new by Jesus Christ. You give Him your sinful nature, and He gives you His righteousness and holiness. You give Him your weakness, and He gives you His power.

Simply pray:

"Jesus, I confess that I have sinned again and again. I feel trapped in addicting habits, but I am reaching out to you in hope and faith. Thank You for dying on the cross for me. Please forgive me and grant me a new start today. I give myself to You and invite You to be Lord of my life. Thank you for saving me from the power of sin and death. Please fill me with Your Holy Spirit and give me your power, wisdom and grace so that I can obey You and walk according to Your ways every moment of every day. Amen."

If you prayed this prayer. Please let us know: rayofhope4u@hotmail.com We would like to send you some resources to help you begin your new relationship with God.

In 1 John 1:8-9, God promises to forgive all our sins if we are honest with Him about our failings. Look at King David. The Bible spares no detail about how this great hero of Israel failed miserably when he was tempted sexually (see 2 Samuel 11:1-12:25). When David should have been on the battlefield with his men, he lingered in Jerusalem and happened to see a beautiful woman bathing on her rooftop. Now, that accidental glimpse was not sin. But he allowed his eyes to linger, and that led to lust, which in turn led to adultery, lies, betrayal, and murder. David fell into the pattern of sin described in James 1:14- 15: "But each one is tempted when, by his own evil desire, he is dragged away and enticed. Then, after desire has conceived, it gives birth to sin; and sin, when it is full- grown, gives birth to death."

Yet David found forgiveness and mercy when he finally stopped pretending that nothing was wrong and humbly repented. Read through his heartfelt prayer in Psalm 51, and consider making it your own:

Psalm 51:1-17 For the director of music. A psalm of David. When the prophet Nathan came to him after David had committed adultery with Bathsheba. Have mercy on me, O God, according to your unfailing love; according to your great compassion blot out my transgressions. Wash away all my iniquity and cleanse me from my sin. For I know my transgressions, and my sin is always before me. Against you, you only, have I sinned and done what is evil in your sight, so that you are proved right when you speak and justified when you judge. Surely I was sinful at birth, sinful from the time my mother conceived me. Surely you desire truth in the inner parts ; you teach me wisdom in the inmost place. Cleanse me with hyssop, and I will be clean; wash me, and I will be whiter than snow. Let me hear joy and gladness; let the bones you have crushed rejoice. Hide your face from my sins and blot out all my iniquity. Create in me a pure heart, O God, and renew a steadfast spirit within me. Do not cast me from your presence or take your Holy Spirit from me. Restore to me the joy of your salvation and grant me a willing spirit, to sustain me. Then I will teach transgressors your ways, and sinners will turn back to you. Save me from bloodguilt, O God, the God who saves me, and my tongue will sing of your righteousness. O Lord, open my lips, and my mouth will declare your praise. You do not delight in sacrifice, or I would bring it; you do not take pleasure in burnt offerings. The sacrifices of God are a broken spirit; a broken and contrite heart, O God, you will not despise.

We can also be encouraged by Paul's example. Although he was a great evangelist and wrote much of the New Testament, Paul struggled with something he called "a thorn in the flesh." After pleading with the Lord to remove it, Paul received an answer that gives us hope for any situation or temptation we may face: "But He said to me, 'My grace is sufficient for you, for My power is made perfect in weakness.'" Paul commented, "Therefore I will boast all the more gladly about my weaknesses, so that Christ's power may rest on me" (2 Corinthians 12:9).

Praise God – we are weak, but He is strong! We may fail, but He will give us a new start every time we humbly come to Him!

Spend Time With God Daily

It's absolutely essential that we look to God for strength and wisdom each day. Spend time reading, studying and meditating on the Scriptures daily. Start with the passages listed below. The Word of God is your spiritual armor, and you dare not enter the battle without it!

Daily prayer is also necessary for victory. James 1:5-6 instructs us: "If any of you lacks wisdom, he should ask God, who gives generously to all without finding fault, and it will be given to him. But when he asks, he must believe and not doubt, because he who doubts is like a wave of the sea, blown and tossed by the wind."

Learn to cry out to God quickly when confronted by trials, temptation, and a desire to yield to addicting behavior. When Peter was sinking in the waves, he prayed one of the shortest prayers in the Bible – "Lord, save me!" – and was immediately rescued by the Lord (see Matthew 14:22-33).

Prayerfully reflect on the names of God which reveal His wonderful character, such as Father, Strong Deliverer, Redeemer, Master, Savior, Mighty God, Helper, Light of the World, Faithful and True, Friend of Sinners, the Way, the Truth, and the Life.

Give yourself entirely to God daily. Romans 12:1b-2a says, "Offer your bodies as living sacrifices, holy and pleasing to God – this is your spiritual act of worship. Do not conform any longer to the pattern of this world, but be transformed by the renewing of your mind."

Rest assured: God will deliver you from sinful habits and addicting behavior if you fully trust Him and do not doubt Him or depend on your own thinking. Sometimes this happens instantaneously, but other times He wants us to walk into victory one small step at a time. This walk of faith is described in Proverbs 3:5-8: "Trust in the Lord with all your heart and lean not on your own understanding; in all your ways acknowledge Him, and He will make your paths straight. Do not be wise in your own eyes; fear the Lord and shun evil. This will bring health to your body and nourishment to your bones."

Choose Your Allies

Although we certainly must go directly to God, confess our sin, and receive forgiveness, there are times that we really need the Body of Christ. Many who have been freed from pornography say they could not win the battle alone. Consider choosing a trusted ally or two to help you gain the victory over addicting habits. Jesus said, "If two of you on earth agree about anything you ask for, it will be done for you by My Father in heaven. For where two or three come together in My name, there am I with them" **(Matthew 18:19-20).**

Going to church on Saturday/Sunday morning is great, but honest one-on-one relationships are also very effective. As long as people hide a dark secret, it can have power over them. But when that secret is shared with a trusted counselor, its power can be broken! **James 5:16 says**, "Therefore confess your sins to each other and pray for each other so that you may be healed. The prayer of a righteous man is powerful and effective."

Of course, it's critically important to find the right person – such as a pastor, counselor, elder, or a very mature Christian friend. It's best if men meet with men and women meet with women. A good mentor demonstrates God's love, mercy and truth while able to ask hard questions, hold a person accountable, and rejoice with each success. Above all, this person must be totally trustworthy and never repeat confidences without a person's permission.

Some people find a great deal of help in overcoming addicting behavior by attending Christian accountability groups that offer confidentiality. **Proverbs 11:14b says, "Many advisers make victory sure."**.

Count The Consequences

"Jerry" is a born-again, Spirit-filled Christian who is happily married to a beautiful, caring woman. He's a good dad to his children, a model schoolteacher, well regarded in the community, and a respected leader in his church. Nevertheless, Jerry struggled long and hard with an addiction to porn – even after counseling sessions with his pastor. But one day, his accountability group asked him to look into the future and describe where his addiction to porn would lead. Thoughtfully, he replied, "Ultimately, I would lose my wife, my family, my home, my job, and my ministry." After taking a long, hard look at the consequences, Jerry decided that pornography simply wasn't worth it – and that helped set him free.

Take time to carefully examine your life and think about what is most precious to you. Then ask yourself, Am I really willing to risk it all?

Identify Your Triggers

It's important to identify exactly what situations trigger you to stumble and fall into addicting activities – such as walking past a magazine rack at the gas station, driving through a certain part of town, staying in a hotel during a business trip, opening the Sunday paper with the lingerie ads, logging on to the Internet, etc. Once you know your weak points, you must be very methodical about avoiding these situations. For example, if you are tempted to watch pornographic movies on cable TV while away on business trips, ask the hotel to disconnect or remove your television before you enter your room. Another good defense is to call a mentor or accountability partner. That person can agree with you in prayer and speak the truth of God's Word, breaking the power of that temptation.

James 4:7 says, Submit yourselves **the**refore to God. **Resist the devil**, and he will flee from you.

If you're married, you may want to enlist your spouse in helping you avoid certain triggers. One man asked his wife to remove all the lingerie sale fliers from the Sunday paper before bringing it into the house. Another man asked his wife to change the password on their computer so he could never log on without her knowledge.

"HALT"

The acronym "HALT" may be helpful, reminding you not to get too **Hungry, Angry, Lonely, or Tired**. Realize that you are more vulnerable to addicting behavior during these times, then HALT – immediately stop what you are doing to pray, read your Bible, and/or call someone for prayer. Of course, you may always call or text +447429721970 for prayer and encouragement.

Dig Out The Roots

Another way to gain victory in the future is to examine your past. If you have never forgiven certain people for hurting you, take time to do it right now! Lack of forgiveness hinders the flow of God's power in our lives. Jesus said, "Therefore I tell you, whatever you ask for in prayer, believe that you have received it, and it will be yours. And when you stand praying, if you hold anything against anyone, forgive him, so that your Father in heaven may forgive you your sins" (Mark 11:24-25).

Sometimes, Christians like to move forward without looking back – but if hurts from the past are preventing wholeness today, it may be helpful to deal with these wounds through prayerful Christian counseling. Truth comes through the Spirit of Christ – and as John 8:32 says, "Then you will know the truth, and the truth will set you free." Also, the books listed at the end of this pamphlet are excellent resources for individual study.

Take Authority Over Your Eyes

Every Man's Battle, by Arterburn, Stoeker and Yorkey, contains practical hints about how to win over sexual temptation. The authors suggest developing the habit of immediately "bouncing your eyes" away from anything that tempts you. If you're watching a great football game on TV and a sexy beer commercial comes on – zap it with your remote instantly! If you're at work and notice that a co-worker's blouse is too low or her skirt is too high, turn away immediately – or look her squarely in the eyes, and nowhere else. Just as you developed a habit of impure thoughts, you can now develop a habit of purity, with God's help.

Grow In God's Word

This teaching is full of powerful Scripture verses to help you grow in spiritual strength and maturity. Take time to look them up and underline them in your Bible, and memorize the ones that are most helpful to you personally. Here are some additional passages to study:

Genesis 39 1 Corinthians 10:12-13

Psalm 51 2 Corinthians 10:3-5

Psalm 119:9-11 Galatians 5:1, 13, 16-18

Proverbs 6:20-24 Ephesians 2:10

Proverbs 23:26-28 Ephesians 5:1-33

Daniel 3 Ephesians 6:10-18

Matthew 26:41 Philippians 4:8

Mark 7:20-23 Colossians 3:1-10

Luke 4:1-12 1 Thessalonians 4:1-8

John 10:10 1 Timothy 6:11-12

John 15:1-17 2 Timothy 2:22

John 17:3 Titus 2:11-14

Acts 15:28-29 1 Peter 2:16

Romans 7:15-8:14 James 1:13-15

Romans 12:1-2 James 4:1-10

Romans 13:12-14 Revelation 2:7

Romans 1:16-32 1 Peter 4:1-6

Romans 6:23 Hebrews 4:15-16

Pray Continually

Prayer is our lifeline to the Savior, who can rescue us from every trial, temptation and addiction. The Bible says, "Pray continually" (1 Thessalonians 5:17). You may wish to be guided by this wonderful prayer that Jesus gave His disciples in Matthew 6:9b-13:

"Our Father in heaven, hallowed be Your name." [Spend time praising God for His love, wisdom and power, and for all that He has done for you.]

"Your kingdom come, Your will be done on earth as it is in heaven." [Ask God to fulfill His marvelous purposes in your life, in the lives of your loved ones, and others].

"Give us today our daily bread." [Pray that you will trust Him to give you the strength you need for every situation you may encounter today. Lift up any other needs you or your family may have.]

"Forgive us our debts, as we also have forgiven our debtors." [Confess any sins you have committed and forgive anyone who has sinned against you.]

"And lead us not into temptation, but deliver us from the evil one." [Ask God to help you obey as He leads you away from the road that leads to evil and destruction and guides you in the paths of righteousness. Spend time listening to His voice speaking in your heart, giving you encouragement, admonition, or instructions. Commit all that you say and do today unto Him.] Amen!

May God bless you as you trust Him each day for strength, wisdom and victory.

Get Involved

I feel one of the best ways to grow in our relationship with God, along with worship, Bible study, and relationships with other God-followers, is to get involved in serving Him. In the Bible, James tells us: **"Do not merely listen to the word, and so deceive yourselves. Do what it says. Anyone who listens to the word but does not do what it says is like a man who looks at his face in a mirror and, after looking at himself, goes away and** immediately forgets what he looks like. But the man who looks intently into the perfect law that gives freedom, and continues to do this, not forgetting what he has heard, but doing it - he will be blessed in what he does." (James 1:22-25)

James understood one big thing about Christians. We love to talk, but we don't necessarily like to get up and out and get it done. It's one thing to proclaim Jesus on Sunday/ Saturday morning. It's quite another to get wrapped up in the lives of others on any given day, for no other reason than to bring a smile to God's face. To maintain freedom you must get involved. Do what the word says...

Anointing breaks the yoke

"20 Command the Israelites to bring you clear oil of pressed olives for the light so that the lamps may be kept burning." (Exodus 27:20) NIV

What is the anointing? The anointing is the very presence of God in our lives. Without the anointing we are powerless and ineffective. In the Old Testament we see many examples of men that were anointed with oil before walking in their call. The Levites were anointed, Saul was anointed before becoming a king; David also was anointed before becoming King. The anointing is the supernatural power that we all need, not only to be able to walk in the call of our ministry effectively, but also in order to be able to carry out the demands of our Christian live. Jesus was and is our example; He is known as Jesus the Christ; the word Christ means: "The anointed one."

In Exodus 27, we see a few hidden secrets concerning this anointing; we must remember that the Old Testament is the shadow of the reality of the New Testament. In this verse, God is talking to Moses and He establishes a few very important points concerning the anointing:

Every believer is responsible for their own anointing:

The anointing can't be delegated. We can't survive out of the anointing of another man; we must pursue that anointing ourselves; we must desire that kind of anointed life. Jesus was more than a miracle worker; Jesus was sinless and perfect. That kind of power is available for each believer. Do you want it?

The anointing is the result of the pressures, pains and tribulations of life: The Bible tells us in this verse: "Command the Israelites to bring you clear oil of hard- pressed olives..." The word press means: "Subject to a lot of pressure and lacking sufficient resources." The anointing will cost you your life; the anointing can't be given to you in seminary or by a big-shot minister laying hands on you in a conference. The anointing comes out of pressure, tribulation, hardship, problems, etc.

We can't be the light of the world if we are not anointed: It is the anointing; that pure oil, that produces the light. It is impossible to be the light of the world if we are lacking the anointing of God.

The anointing can't be a one-day or once-in-a-while thing; the anointing must be a daily thing: The Bible tells us here that: "the lamps may be kept burning." This is a typology of the way we ought to go after God and after the power of His anointing. Every day we ought to live powerful lives; that is the example of Christ for the whole world.

Without the anointing we can't learn Spiritual principles: First John 2:27 tells us: "27 But the anointing which you have received from Him abides in you, and you do not need that anyone teach you; but as the same anointing teaches you concerning all things, and is true, and is not a lie, and just as it has taught you, you will abide in Him." NKJV

The word anointing here is the word chrísma, this is where we get the word christós or "Christ" meaning: The Anointed One; it stands for the Holy Spirit.

It is the anointing that destroy the yokes: Isaiah 10:27"It shall come to pass in that day That his burden will be taken away from your shoulder,
And his yoke from your neck,

And the yoke will be destroyed because of the anointing oil." NKJV Only the anointing makes our ministries effective; it is the anointing that make people free.

Talents are irrevocable, but the anointing can be taken away from us due to rebelliousness: 1Samuel 15:23-26

"23 For rebellion is as the sin of witchcraft, And stubbornness is as iniquity and idolatry. Because you have rejected the word of the Lord, He also has rejected you from being king." Then Saul said to Samuel, "I have sinned, for I have transgressed the commandment of the Lord and your words, because I feared the people and obeyed their voice. 25 Now therefore, please pardon my sin, and return with me, that I may worship the Lord."26 But Samuel said to Saul, "I will not return with you, for you have rejected the word of the Lord, and the Lord has rejected you from being king over Israel." NKJV

Beloved, we need the anointing; it is essential in our Christian lives; it is the power to learn, it is the power to do, the power to say, the power to resist, the power to stay, the power to overcome, the power to leave, the power of restoration, the power to speak, the power to sing, the power to be quiet, the power to confront, the power to overcome, the power to move forward, the power to write, and the power to be all that God has call us to be.

Prayer This Prayer

If you have never asked Jesus to be your Lord and Savior and don't know how, it's easy. It's so simple that many people think it can't be for real . . . but it is! God knew that not one of us would be able to personally make up for the things He doesn't want us to do. This is called sinning or rebelling against God. So He sent His Son Jesus to pay the penalty for the sins of every person once and for all.

For all have sinned and fall short of the glory of God, and are justified freely by his grace through the redemption that came by Christ Jesus. (Rom. 3:23)

While this may be hard for you to understand just now, all you need to do is believe that Jesus died for you, confess to God that there is sin in your life, and accept His forgiveness and His gift of eternal life.

Don't wait another moment, pray this prayer right now and put God in charge of your life:

Dear Lord Jesus, I believe that You are the Son of God. I believe that You died for my sins and rose from the grave. I invite You into my heart and receive You right now. Thank You for forgiveness. Thank You for a new life. Help me to be what You want me to be and live your life through me. Amen.

Have you invited Jesus Christ to be your Lord and Savior? Email me on rayofhope4u@hotmail.com You have just made the most important decision of your life by accepting Jesus Christ as your Lord and Savior. With Him by your side, you are ready to face the road ahead. And you can face it with the assurance of God's promise: And we know that in all things God works for the good of those who love him, who have been called according to his purpoзc. (Rom. 8:28)

Further Reading & Resources

How to Deal with Your Sexual Addiction. More tools for your toolbox

If you find yourself engulfed in a sexual addiction, here are some general tips that have helped many of us on our journey toward restoration and healing:

1. Face the facts

"For all have sinned and fall short of the glory of God" (Romans 3:23). There are many ways that we humans sin and fall short— lying, greed, stealing, adultery, taking the Lord's name in vain, and many other selfish acts. All sins are equally serious before our Holy God. If there is some sexual sin in your life, the first step toward improvement is to admit what you have done. If you have given yourself to pornography, sexual fantasies or cheating involving people other than your spouse, you have been committing adultery. Jesus said: "You have heard that it was said to those of old, 'You shall not commit adultery.' "But I say to you that whoever looks at a woman or man to lust for her has already committed adultery with her in his heart" (Matthew 5:27-28). Grasp the seriousness of this. You have been breaking a commandment of God. You have turned something beautiful (sex), into something ugly, selfish and damaging. If you are married, then you have been unfaithful to your spouse. If single, you are sinning against the dear person you may one day marry. If you are returning to this behavior over and over again, despite your desire to stop, then you are out control. You are addicted. If this is the case, and you can admit it, then congratulations; you have taken the first step toward recovery.

2. Spiritual Salvation

The single biggest factor in combatting such an addiction is to come under the authority of Jesus Christ. You are involved in a spiritual battle. If you are not yet a Christian, we strongly urge you to confess your sin and totally surrender your life to Him. Accept His gift of eternal salvation for your soul. After accepting Christ, some are totally delivered from their addictions. If there is no doubt that you have already committed your life to Jesus Christ and are relying on His sin-covering blood for your salvation, then Instead, deal with your sin. Confess it, and rededicate your life to Christ. **do not let your sin cause you to doubt your salvation.** Don't hold back any part of your life from Him because He already knows. Humble yourself totally before God. Surrender it all. Ask Him to help you live a life of purity and true love. Accept your own failure and inadequacy. Admit that you cannot overcome sin on your own. The apostle Paul understood the frustration and terrible hold that our inherited sin has on all descendants of Adam and Eve: "I do not understand what I do. For what I want to do I do not do, but what I hate I do. And if I do what I do not want to do, I agree that the law is good. ...I know that nothing good lives in me, that is, in my sinful nature. For I have the desire to do what is good, but I cannot carry it out. For what I do is not the good I want to do; no, the evil I do not want to do—this I keep on doing. Now if I do what I do not want to do, it is no longer I who do it, but it is sin living in me that does it. So I find this law at work: When I want to do good, evil is right there with me. For in my inner being I delight in God's law; but I see another law at work in the members of my body, waging war against the law of my mind and making me a prisoner of the law of sin at work within my members. What a wretched man I am! Who will rescue me from this body of death?" —Romans 7:15-24 (NIV)

3. Admit your weakness, seek God's help

All humans are selfish and sinful; it is our nature. Addiction to pornography and other sexual sins are particularly potent in their effect, similar to a seductive and powerful drug. Once it has a hold on you, it is very difficult to resist. In fact, it is impossible to overcome on your own. You must have God's help. God cannot work with you if you are still trying to overcome sin on your own; it is a form of pridefulness. You are, in effect, saying to God "I can take care of this myself." Consider these verses: "The wicked in his proud countenance does not seek God..." (Psalm 10:4). "Pride goes before destruction..." (Proverbs 16:18). "When pride comes, then comes shame; But with the humble is wisdom" (Proverbs 11:2). "You will keep him in perfect peace, Whose mind is stayed on You, Because he trusts in You" (Isa 26:3, NKJV).**"Therefore humble yourselves**

under the mighty hand of God, that He may exalt you in due time, casting all your care upon Him, for He cares for you" (I Peter 5:6-7). You see, God's willingness to "exalt you" (lift you up spiritually) is dependent on your willingness to humble yourself before Him. But the second part is just as important: God cares for you so much that He is willing to take all of your cares (worries, anxieties, needs, fears, desires, challenges, regrets, etc.) upon Himself. In other words, humble yourself by accepting your inability to handle the cares of life and give them all over to God. THEN He will lift you up spiritually, and you will find peace and freedom unlike anything you've ever known. The Holy Spirit will be the most powerful in your life, when you are the most humble— when you get your own interests and desires out of the way. Then, He can produce in you the fruit He promised: love, joy, peace, patience, kindness, goodness, faithfulness, gentleness, and self control (Galatians 5:22-23). Notice that last one—self control. It is important to see that self-control is not simply a matter of one's will; it is, in fact, a fruit of the Holy Spirit (a gift) working in us. What a merciful God we have! As we learn to depend more and more on God to see us through each day, and we become more aware of His presence moment by moment, we find that over time the magnet of sexual sin loses its strength.

4. The power of Prayer

Prayer is conversation with our Creator. It is a child's communion with his Father. The Bible emphasizes that it should have a very high priority in our lives. Continual prayer is very important to your recovery Eph 6:18. If there was ever a time in your life when you need to pray, it is now. It is the Christian's greatest weapon against the sin nature and the dangers and temptations of this world. "Anything of value in the kingdom of God is initiated in and dependent on prayer." Rely on God, and learn to think as He does. This will bring a revolution of good in your life. Here's how to pray, each and every day for total deliverance from sin including your addiction.

- Confess all sin Read: Psalm 51 | Mark 7:20-23 | 1 John 1:7- 10
- Renounce conformity to the world Read: Romans 12:2, 6:13- 14
- Ardently seek an intimate relationship with Jesus Christ. He

will give you a richer, more meaningful life. Read: John 10:10, 15:5-12 | Ephesians 3:14-19 | Philippians 3:10-14
- Offer your body as a "living sacrifice" to God See: Romans 12:1-2 | 1 Corinthians 6:19-20
- Worship God Read: John 4:23-24 | Philippians 3:3 | Mark 5:6
- Thank and praise God. Thank Him for his grace and mercy, praise Him, and keep seeking His mercy. Thank God for answered prayer. Read: What should we thank God for, and how should we praise Him? | Thanksgiving, do the right thing | Are you thankful to God? | Philippians 4:6-7 | Colossians

4:2

- Ask God for help in living a pure and loving lifeSee:

Philippians 4:6-7 | Hebrews 4:16

5. Reading and memorizing God's Promises Memorizing scripture is an often overlooked weapon that should be in every Christian's arsenal. Memorize James 1:14 and 1 Corinthians 10:13

and quote them when you are tempted. Open your Bible at Psalm 51 and make it your own prayer. The following passages are also helpful in dealing with lust and sexual immorality:

Matthew 5:27-30 | 1 Peter 2:11 | Romans 8:13 | Romans 6:12 | 1 Corinthians 6:13 | Galatians 5:17 | Philippians 4:8 | 2 Timothy 2:22 | Psalm 101:2,3 | Proverbs 6:25-29 | Proverbs 5:18-20 | Proverbs 8:13 | Job 31:1-4 | Matthew 5:8 | Romans 8:6 | 1 Corinthians 6:9 | 1 Corinthians 6:18-19 | 2 Corinthians 10:5, 1 Thessalonians 4:3-5 | James 1:15; 4:3 | 1 John 2:16

Not only should Scripture memory be a regular part of your life as a Christian, reading the Bible regularly should as well. Read the Bible daily, without fail.

6. Accountability

Although you may be ashamed of the sins you are involved in, don't let that shame become one of Satan's weapons to keep you trapped. Secrecy is often a Christian's biggest enemy, while confession can bring freedom and release from the bondage of an overwhelming sense of shame. If no one knows of your personal moral failures, there is no one to be accountable to, or to help lift you up in prayer or encourage you. Don't let your pride destroy you (Prov. 29:23; Mark 7:21; 2 Chr, 32:26). In an accountability relationship, you choose a confidant that you can be honest and open with about your addiction. Confess your sin (James 5:16). Be sure to choose someone of the same sex. Preferably, select a discrete person that has some spiritual maturity in their walk with Christ, and who has a helpful, non-condemning spirit.Some of you maybe church leaders or teachers. We fully understand that breaking total secrecy about your sin is going to be especially difficult. But it is still necessary. God requires more of shepherds (not less) and holds them more accountable. Trust God and pray about who He would have assist you. Humble yourself. Proceed with wisdom and faith. Do what needs to be done. As a leader, it is even more important for you to do what is right and to deal decisively with your sin. If your addiction involves viewing Internet pornography, there is an Internet service that can assist you. **Covenant Eyes.net is an on- line accountability service**. They point out that "while Internet filters can provide some help, they can also block acceptable web sites, creating frustration. Filters can also be turned off or **bypassed, rendering them ineffective**. The Covenant Eyes Program removes the secrecy and privacy of using the Internet. Covenant Eyes promotes self-control and personal discipline, and the individual is held accountable in their Internet use." It works by logging the address of each Web site visited, then compiling a list of visited sites that can be viewed on-line by your accountability partner. Users often find their temptation dramatically reduced and often leave it altogether once they know someone is monitoring their Web usage.

If you spend much time on the Internet, computer monitoring (as mentioned above with Covenant Eyes) or Internet filters are highly recommended. There are many filters to choose from, including:

AFA Filter—single profile, with no password overrides. This means no guessed or cracked passwords, resulting in maximum protection for children and adults. See: AFAfilter.com

Hedgebuilders—free to pastors, missionaries, and Christian schools. Others pay a small fee. See: Hedge.org

7. Guard your heart, avoid temptations

Guard your heart with all diligence (Proverbs 4:23). Don't let the demonic realm influence your thought-life (Ephesians 6:12-20). If you give yourself to sinful fantasies and pursuits, you will become their slave (Romans 6:16). **A simple change of habit can do wonders in keeping you from temptation.** For example, if you are most tempted when you spend time on the computer after your spouse has gone to bed, then make a commitment to stay off of the computer during that time. Go to bed with her. If you know that a certain street you drive down causes you to lust due to certain establishments on it, or prostitutes that hang around, or alluring billboards, you would be wise to travel a different route. "Turn my eyes away from worthless things; preserve my life according to your word" (Psalm 119:37). Stephen Arterburn in his book Every Man's Battle talks about retraining the eyes to "bounce away" from visual things that stimulate lust in you. For men, this might mean you need to look away as soon as you see a scantily dressed female jogger. Don't fuel your lust. Avert your eyes from temptations, and don't look back.The same applies to visual temptations on magazines at the grocery store checkout line, or billboards, television programming and commercials. A good habit can be formed in around two weeks. Keep bouncing your gaze away, and remarkable improvement can be noticed rather quickly.

8. **Destroy all Paraphernalia (pornographic materials etc) in your possession**—magazines, books, videos, and computer files. Make no provision for your flesh (Romans 13:14). If you can't control yourself, then you must then get rid of every possible access to pornographic material in your life (Internet, cable TV, etc.). Stop feeding the fire. **If some friendships cause too much temptation, severe those relationships.** 1 Corinthians 15:33, NKJV

A Love Letter to My Porn-Loving Spouse By Anonymous

Dear Spouse,

When we stood before God, took our vows to love, honour and cherish each other, for better or worse, till death do we part - I truly believe we both meant it. Never in a million years did I think that a few years later I'd be in the position I find myself in today.

So many aspects of our life are so wonderful: our children, going places together, getting together with friends, our jobs, and other happy things. But when you are alone with your computer or your super-duper cell phone, you feed a very dark side of you that has grown like a cancer. It's your love affair with porn.

I thought maybe a letter would be the best way to tell you how I feel because when I've talked to you about this, I've felt like you have minimized your involvement, gotten on the defensive and avoided really hearing my heart. I refuse to nag. I refuse to live in denial. I refuse to be hurt repeatedly.

I love you. I love you just as much as I ever have. But I am hurting. I feel betrayed when I know that you are lusting over someone else. I feel abandoned when I go to bed alone and you are in your private world with your computer. I feel repulsion when I happen to pass by and see what you're spending your time with. I feel despised when I hear you respond to my questions about your behaviour. I feel tainted when we make love. These are not feelings that I want to continue to feel. They are painful.

If I've learned anything in life, it's that I can't change another person. I choose to love you because you are my spouse. I choose to seek an emotionally healthy environment because I believe God wants to use me to carry out his will for my life. He tells me that he has plans for me that are good and not for disaster, to give me a future and a hope. He has those same plans for you, but porn's not part of them.

I want you to be freed from this evil that has snuck into our lives. I have prayed for this for many months now. I will continue to pray for you to be released. I will lift you up before the Lord day and night because I love you. However, I will be doing this from a different dwelling.

You have made your choice. I am still going to love, honour and cherish you, for better or worse (which this is the worse), till death do we part. I hope you will do all that you can to stop feeding this addiction that has brought us to this place. I am not parting from you; I am putting physical distance between us for my own survival. The children are coming with me and I will be glad to work out fair visitation for you. The crazy thing is—I know that if you saw me physically getting hurt repeatedly, you'd do anything you could to stop that from happening to me. But there's a disconnect when it comes to my emotional pain. I feel unloved in that regard. I'm going to seek comfort from the Lord and look to Him to be the source of my healing. We are both Christians and both know the Lord can make all things new. I'm starting my new "me" today. I hope you will start your new "you" someday also. When you do, come find me. I'll be ready to feel loved, honoured and cherished again.

I truly love you and the Lord, Your Spouse

A Pastor's Struggle With Sex and Porn Addiction

On a cold winter night in 1994, in the grip of a decades-long addiction to porn and illicit sex, I began my typical ritual of acting out sexually. I sat in a familiar parking lot of a XXX bookstore, unusually troubled by the routine I was about to perform even though I had carried it out too many times to count. I had a beautiful wife at home, but she was the last thing on my mind.

Less than a block from the porn shop sat a century old cathedral. Without warning, an impulse to set foot in that house of worship overwhelmed me. I walked toward the edifice, hiked the tall steps, and opened the monolithic oak doors. I sat in the back row of pews, the silence was terrifying. In that space, I reconnected with something I had lost– my true self. The part of me that wanted more than compulsion, shame, and despair.

That evening was the beginning of the end. Only a few months later, my wife caught me in a lie, and my double life was completely exposed.

"What are you doing home so early?" my wife asked me as I walked through the front door.

"I just decided to come home," I answered. "But you just told me on the phone that you got called out on a job," she continued.

The puzzled look on her face told me she wanted to know more. I had called my wife to say I was working late. I wasn't. My scheme was to launch into my ritual of cruising for sex. But something made me change my mind. My wife was more than a little surprised when only twenty minutes later, I walked into our apartment.

"I said I might be working late." Now I was contradicting what I had actually said. This was the first time in as long as I could remember that I hadn't prepared an alibi.

"Either you got called out or you didn't. There's no maybe. Which is it?"

The blood drained from my face and my mouth went dry. "What I meant to say is–is–is that I would . . . be home late, but that I, I was le-leaving the office right then." I hoped that she wasn't noticing my perspiring forehead. "I had to take care of some things," I explained, praying she would let it go and change the subject.

"Michael, what's going on?" There was no use continuing the charade. She caught me. The dam holding back the lies and deceit burst. "I didn't get called out," I mumbled.

"Then why did you say you did? What were you doing?"

After what seemed like hours of silence, I spoke the words my wife has dreaded ever since. "There is something I have to tell you . . ." For the next several hours I poured out my secret life: porn, prostitutes, people and places she knew nothing about. To say Julianne was devastated would be an understatement. She was in shock, betrayed, confused, angry. I slept on the floor that night . . . and many nights following, as she cried herself to sleep behind a locked bedroom door.

July 10, 1994, was the worst day of my life. It was the day on which I unleashed a hurricane of destruction and was forced to watch the woman I loved crawl in the wreckage. When I was single, my actions didn't immediately affect anyone in my circle of family and friends. Now the consequences of my recklessness could be seen in Julianne's eyes. I had caused my wife's worst nightmare to come

It was also the best day of my life. Though I was shattered, it was the day I finally understood Jesus' words recorded in the gospel of John: the truth shall set you free.

My own addiction to porn and illicit sex began in high school. No matter how close I came to getting caught, I always managed to jump in the manure and come out smelling like a rose. While working in church ministry in my mid-twenties, my addiction was nearly exposed in a newspaper story about a raid on an escort service. But even that didn't lead to change. I might stop for a time, vow to mend my ways, tear up my porn magazines, but eventually the insatiable urge would return.

Now, I've been counselling men with pornography and sex addictions for more than twenty years.

In my line of work, barely a day goes by that I don't hear a story about a man or woman who has lost something dear– their marriage, family relationships, job, ministry, reputation, self-respect– because of pornography. Of course, when we experience such loss, it also affects spouses, children, friends, congregations, and communities. Everyone loses when it comes to porn.

It's tempting to think that there's nothing wrong with a porn habit that no one gets hurt. We think we're protecting our spouse by not telling them. We think we're providing ourselves with a respite from a stressful day. No matter how we justify or rationalize it, in two decades of counselling, not one (person) has told me that pornography made them a better husband, wife, father, parent, employee, or friend.

My message to those who are in the snares of sexual compulsion is two fold. First, you can be free and whole. Trying to manage and white knuckle this issue is not as good as it gets. Others have walked a trusted path to healing and recovery, you can too. Start by deciding you will come out of the shadows and into the light. Talk with a friend, professional counsellor, or Twelve-Step Group like Sex Addicts Anonymous.

Second, sexual compulsions are not actually about sex. Almost a century ago, G. K. Chesterton wrote that the man who knocks on the brothel door is knocking for God. If he were writing today, he might say that the man who surfs online for porn is surfing for God. Consider what the Apostle Paul wrote in Corinthians: "sex is more than mere skin on skin. It is as much spiritual mystery as physical fact." (1 Corinthians 6:16, MSG).

Beyond bodies seeking and experiencing sexual pleasure – all of us reach toward some spiritual mystery we cannot see, touch, or comprehend physically. Maybe this is why describe great sex as "spiritual," and utter "Oh God!" during climax. To deny the spiritual hunger hidden within the sexual impulse is to set ourselves up for a never-ending cycle that only leads to desperation, despair, and bondage.

God is not mad at you if you are struggling with sexual compulsion. In fact, that secret, hidden place of your greatest struggle, failure or shame is exactly where God wants to meet you and give you a great gift. I should know. It happened to me.

A Letter To Women

The following copyrighted excerpt is reprinted with permission from the author, Ezra Snyder, *Becoming Unbound: From Pornography to Freedom,* © 2011. ───────────

This is a letter written by my wife, Heather, to any woman who has just learned that her man is struggling or has struggled with pornography or other area of sexual purity.

Dear Beloved,

If you are reading this, your man has just made a confession that has broken your heart. There is a hole in your chest that wasn't there before and things feel like they may never be the same again. And it's possible this isn't the first time. I am so sorry. I don't know the exact details of your story, but I do know your pain. I am truly sorry that you have found yourself in this place. This is not how things were meant to be. You were created for something far greater, and so was your man. You were both designed to live in perfect freedom – from pain, from heartache, and from the effects of pornography. That freedom may seem far away as you read this letter. I understand. But there is hope.

When Ezra first told me that he struggled with pornography I felt like I was going to throw up. It was literally revolting to me and I could hardly even look at him – except perhaps to check my aim before I tried to kick him. We had been married less than a year and I could hardly believe this was happening. Instead of hearing my husband sharing a struggle with me, I heard all sorts of other things: *You cannot trust your husband. He is weak. He has betrayed you. This is your fault. If you were a better wife, he wouldn't have turned to porn. You will never be enough for him.* He may as well have handed me a report card on my performance as a wife with a big, old, fatty "**F**" marked across the top. How could I have failed so completely as a wife? As a woman?

Over the next eight years those lies wove their way into the daily world of our marriage. Every time Ezra would tell me that he had screwed up and looked at porn again, the lies were reinforced. He confessed three or four times after the first night. In my mind, he became weaker and weaker and less and less worthy of my respect. I felt that my failure as a wife and a woman was confirmed time and time again. Despite this, each time he confessed and asked for forgiveness, I believed it was definitely the last time. Out of blind hope and ignorance, I did my best to move on as if the problem were solved. I became "Heather the ostrich" with my head firmly entrenched in the sand. Maybe you can relate to this method of dealing with difficult situations. In truth, nothing had been solved. I had no understanding of what was really going on with Ezra. Or just how pervasive a man's struggle with pornography can be. During the early years of our marriage, I had no idea that – depending on which study you choose to believe – 75% to 80% of married, Christian men struggle with some kind of pornography at least once per week. I thought it was an issue that only really creepy guys had to deal with. Some part of me knew that men were visually oriented, but it never occurred to me that a man's battle with pornography would last from very early in life until he's pushing up daisies. I am not sharing this to excuse your man's actions. They were wrong and almost certainly sinful and they have deeply hurt you. I am sharing this because maybe you are like I was – unaware of how big this issue really is.

Ezra finally experienced true freedom from his addiction to pornography on July 22, 2005. As he shared with me a few days later, I could clearly see that it was a different man who sat me down to share exactly what his struggle had looked like through his life and our marriage. He spoke with honesty and humility that I hadn't seen before. He didn't make empty promises. He told me he knew I'd need some time to process this, that he expected me to be angry and that was okay. It took incredible courage for him to do this. I'm guessing it felt a little bit like standing in front of an angry bull with a red shirt on. It took great courage for your man to tell you of his struggle with pornography as well.

I have to tell you that I was pretty pissed off after he told me. Ah, were you expecting me to say I was happy that he was finally free? But, you see, I had no idea that Ezra's struggles were as extensive as they had been. It felt like a bomb being dropped on me. I was ANGRY that he had kept such a pervasive issue from me. And, honestly, the most difficult part was that he was sharing from a place of healing – he had been freed. Freed from something I hadn't realized had been binding him so completely. But that left me in the dust. I wanted to rant at the man who had brought this garbage into our marriage, but part of me knew *that guy* no longer existed. It was like he took my ammo away and that *really* ticked me off.

I don't want to kid you – working through my feelings and our relationship was a long process and it was no cakewalk. It was a full year before I began to trust Ezra fully again, after what felt like a sustained betrayal over the past nine years of marriage. It was closer to two years before I began to learn how to respect him. Very slowly, my picture of my husband began to change from a weak, sex-obsessed man to a strong, trustworthy man of God whose heart toward me was good. Ezra kept pursuing me during these years. Every few weeks he would ask me where I was at with our conversation, how I was feeling about his past struggles with porn, how I was feeling about him and our marriage. Even though I sometimes had trouble articulating my feelings, I loved that he kept pursuing me. He was committed to working through this thing *with* me. Part of me hated that he kept bringing it up, but he was probably just remembering my ostrich tendencies.

One of the most difficult things to work through was the lie that Ezra looking at porn was my fault. That I somehow wasn't enough to satisfy him, so he turned elsewhere. But let me tell you in no uncertain terms – IT IS NOT YOUR FAULT. I understand how it may feel like your fault, but it is not. In fact, your man's struggle has nothing to do with you, dear sister. I understand this may be hard for you to hear right now. This book is about all the reasons men struggle with porn. If you want more insight into your man, read Part II of this book, starting with Chapter Seven. It took me a while, but I finally arrived at a place where I understood that Ezra's struggles with pornography were because of his issues.

Something that also helped me during this time is that Ezra was open with me about his struggles. If he was tempted to look at porn, he shared that struggle with me. This openness took some getting used to. At first, I often felt instant terror: *Did he do it again?* But I chose to listen to Ezra and not my fear. This was crucial in my coming to trust him again. That kind of open dialogue helped rebuild the trust that had been broken during the early years of our marriage.

There is a lot more to this story than I am able to share with you here. The bigger picture involves what I learned about the heart of a woman and the heart of a man – how we were each designed and how our designs played into Ezra's and my life together. There are more resources available to you. I would recommend to you the book *Captivating* by John and Stasi Eldredge if you are interested in understanding your own heart and how God designed you. A book that will give you insight into your man is *Wild at Heart*, also by John Eldredge. And for specific understanding about men and pornography, read this book, *Becoming Unbound*.

I know you have probably just found out that your man struggles with porn and you are dealing with a lot of emotions right now. You may feel like you marriage is over, and it could be if you choose that. You could choose not to forgive him for his sins against you. But I would like to offer you a different option – an option richer and infinitely more rewarding. You can choose to press in. Fight *for* your man. Whether you realize it yet or not, you have great power to speak life into your husband. At this moment, what I'm offering you may seem difficult or even impossible, but I have found in my own marriage that being on Ezra's side has been absolutely worth it. If you choose to fight for your man and for your marriage, here are the most powerful tools I know of to keep in your handbag.

Believe in him. The number one thing you can do for your man is to believe in him. That's right. Believe in him at this moment after he has betrayed your trust. Believe in him even if he screws up. It sounds difficult, right? But one of the core things a man needs is respect. The heart of respect is your believing that he has what it takes, that he can do it. That in the clutch, he can come through. And you can't fake this. He can sniff out a fake sentiment in a heartbeat. Do you think he can remember to buy milk without a reminder? Do you think he can find his way without stopping for directions? Do you believe that he can be free from pornography? If you don't, he'll know it. He'll feel like a failure, a loser who has let you down again. But if you do believe in him he'll see it in your face and hear it in your words. Then he'll go out and conquer the world.

I actually had to ask Ezra to tell me when he felt I was being disrespectful to him – with some caveats on *how* to tell me in a way I could receive, of course! I was honestly not aware of that my actions were disrespectful a lot of the time. Perhaps you aren't either. Often it did not make any sense to me what he saw as disrespectful – my girl brain just doesn't work the same way. But, it doesn't have to. The only thing that needs to make sense is your decision to believe in your man.

Don't try to manage him. You may be tempted to manage your man by trying to control his situation. Perhaps you secretly check up on his computer activity or install a filter behind his back or call him to "innocently" check-in a bit more often. This is absolutely the worst possible thing you can do. Let me ask you a question. How do you feel when someone is trying to manage you? Now, perhaps you are nicer than I am, but I start kicking and screaming (literally and figuratively) pretty quickly. Magnify that by about four million, and you have the average man's reaction. Being managed goes against a man's design. His wild heart is meant to lead. Any attempt to control or manage my man *always* backfires in a hurry.

Don't withhold sex. Another thing you may be tempted to do is to withhold yourself sexually from your husband. Believe me, I tried it and it backfired. Keeping sex as a tool to punish your husband is a sin according to 1 Corinthians 7:5 (NIV). It is also not helpful in any way and will only serve to worsen your marriage. Men receive love two ways – through respect and sex. Keeping sex from your husband will not punish him or teach him not to look at porn, it will only make him feel deeply rejected and unloved. Do not hear me say that you need to go have sex with your husband tonight. There may be some serious consequences of his poor decisions. It's possible he's been unfaithful in a way that needs medical intervention, testing, or health care before you are intimate with him again.

Again, I'm not talking (necessarily) about tonight. I'm talking about the next part of your journey toward a deeper relationship and a better marriage.

Learn about what he's dealing with. If you want to know what it's like to be a man who struggles with pornography, if you want to understand your man better, learn about what he's dealing with. Read this book. Part I is the story of Ezra's personal struggle, told in as frank a way as possible. Part II details Ezra's journey toward freedom. These chapters will shine a light on what your man has been dealing with and the freedom that is available to him (and you).

Walk with him in it. Be his partner in his struggle with pornography. That looks like listening to him when he wants to talk about how he's feeling and how things are going for him. In the beginning I had a difficult time listening to Ezra without getting upset and hearing unintended blame in his words. This was a journey for me, but today we can talk openly about how things are going for him. And that's crucial for him because it means that I understand that the journey has ups and downs. Our men may screw up, they may have some difficult habits to break, but with our help the battle will be easier.

Your man's struggle with pornography is a difficult and painful thing. But you have already taken the first step in the journey to fight for him. You chose to read this letter instead of throwing the book at him. Good work. After five years of fighting for Ezra, my marriage is better than it ever has been. Ezra and I are far from perfect, but we are definitely in this together. You will have to take your own journey and no doubt it will look different than mine. One thing I know is that if you choose to fight for your man and seek God together, you will find your way to a stronger marriage and a greater love for your God and your man.

You can do this. I believe in you. My heart is for you and I will be fighting alongside you through prayer.

"Is Masturbation A Sin?"

Some points to ponder:

Someone asked me this question on Facebook. We know there is a growing pornography industry in our country and all over the world. People in today's society wait longer to get married than ever before. Since sexual temptation usually steps into our lives at puberty we need to address the concerns of those who face the temptation to masturbate when they are unmarried and without a partner or maybe in a messed up marriage. This topic is typically taboo in most social circles and especially Christian social circles.

What Does the Bible Say?

The bible doesn't mention masturbation as a sin not once in its content. It does say that one of the fruits of the Spirit is self-control. I believe that some of the reasons the bible doesn't mention masturbation is because it was written in a time when young men and women got married as soon as puberty hit. Also the lack of stimuli (technology etc) and polygamy. In our times we could be waiting until we're forty or older to get married. Some people put off marriage because they are late bloomers or because they haven't found someone compatible yet - whatever the reason the temptation to find an outlet to sexual energy is there. It could be the bible covers it in Lust the key ingredient in masturbation. Matt 5:28, Prov 23:7 Gen 2:16-17 James 4:1-4 Rom7:14-25 1 Cor 6::9-10 Rom 6:12-23; Jam 4:5-8 .

Fornication, Lust, and Adultery

I believe that masturbation is a type of fornication according to the bible. But since it is not specifically mentioned in the bible I think the best way to find out if it is a sin is to ask God. If the Holy Spirit convicts you that it is wrong it will give you the power to avoid it. If it were a sin we have confidence that God forgives all sins when we repent and turn from them. I want to emphasize the importance of listening to the Holy Spirit in this matter. Jesus says that if a man looks at a woman in lust he has already committed adultery with her in his heart. Both adultery and fornication are sins. Just to be clear, fornication is sex outside of a marital relationship. "As a man thinks so is he". What crosses your mind while masturbating? This will determine weather it's sin.

Sex in the Context of Marriage

Sex is meant to be a means of reproduction and of bonding for a married couple. It is meant to bring us closer and more intimate with our partners. Sex in the context of marriage is never a sin because we were designed to have intimate relationships with the opposite sex. It is part of the union between a man and a woman.

How to Avoid It

It is very important to stay away from things that trigger temptation such as pornography, alcohol, strip clubs, etc. For some people, they do not feel a temptation to masturbate because either they have a spouse or they are exercising self-control, a fruit of the Holy Spirit. The temptation to masturbate is not a sin because it may not be acted upon. With the Holy Spirit we have a choice as to whether or not we will or won't. The best way to make sure you don't overstep the boundaries God has set for sexuality is to pray to God to take the temptation away and to stop giving in to it when it comes.

Exercise a way of fighting temptation

There are many things that you can do to alleviate the pressure you feel to masturbate. Exercise of any type is very good for the body and it can generate some of the same endorphins that sex can. Also, try not to meditate or think about sex so much. Once you get all the sources of sexually explicit content out of your life you will find this a much easier prospect. It is like any other temptation. The bible tells us to submit to God and to resist the devil and he will flee from you. If you don't feel godly masturbating it is a sure sign that you need to stop. The Holy Spirit will convict you.

God's Word

"Don't love the world or anything that belongs to the world. If you love the world, you cannot love the Father. Our foolish pride comes from this world, and so do our selfish desires and our desire to have everything see. None of this comes from the Father. The world and the desires it causes are disappearing.

But if we obey God, we will live forever" (1John 2:15- 17). (1Cor 10:13).

Pray with me

"Dear Heavenly Father, I can't deal with lust apart from you. Please forgive me and cleanse me from my sin. And please replace my lustful desires with Your desires for my life, so that I can glorify You in everything I do. Thank You. In Jesus' name, Amen"

I hope this information will help someone. It wasn't long ago I used to struggle with this temptation, too, but God has helped me to stay away from it. Lets pray for each other

Resources, Reference & Recommended books

Every Man's Battle

Stephen Arterburn, Fred Stoeker, Mike Yorkey Winning the War on Sexual Temptation One Victory at a Time — Shares the stories of dozens who have escaped the trap of sexual immorality (pornography, adultery, etc.) and presents a practical, detailed plan for recovery / This book is designed for both men and women. Men, have you ever said in frustration, "I just can't get free of this sexual sin! Since I'm a man, I guess I'm just doomed to live this way." Wives, have you ever asked, "Why is it that my husband seems to think about sex so much more than I do?" Or, "If sex is so natural, why is it that I've been married 15 years and still have no real sexual intimacy with my husband?" Find the answers you need

When Good Men Are Tempted
(updated edition)
by Bill Perkins A frank and realistic strategy for men to regain purity in the midst of a culture fraught with sexual temptations. Complete with "take action" steps, this book is a must for every man! The author (a pastor) candidly discusses his own struggles with sexual temptation and his desire to stay pure. He provides a biblical and practical strategy for victory. Wives, this book has helped many women understand their mates' temptations and struggles.

Every Heart Restored

A wife's guide to healing in the wake of a husband's sexual sin by Fred and Brenda Stoeker with Mike Yorkey, with Foreword by Stephen Arterburn Are you the wife of a man who is addicted to lust, pornography, or masturbation? If so, you are not alone. This is the book for every woman who has become a casualty in the fight for sexual purity. Every Heart Restored offers godly guidance and wisdom for any woman facing such personal betrayal. Filled with stories from wives and husbands at every stage in the struggle for sexual purity, Every Heart Restored addresses the questions and real-life issues that matter to you most

The Silent War: Ministering to Those Trapped in the Deception of Pornography
by Henry J. Rogers A lifeline in a world in love with evil. Offers hope to thousands of people trapped in secret sin. Pastors and counselors find it very helpful in better understanding and dealing with this very common problem. Endorsed by many Christian leaders

At the Alter of Sexual Idolatry by Steve Gallagher (based on biblical counseling / founder of Pure Life Ministries which deals with sexual sin)

Breaking Free: Understanding Sexual Addiction & the Healing Power of Jesus by Russell Willingham and Bob Davies (good, biblical treatment of sexual addiction)

Faithful and True: Sexual Integrity in a Fallen World by Mark Laaser (a former pastor who was trapped in sexual addiction and recovered) (workbook also available)

False Intimacy: Understanding the Struggle of Sexual Addiction by Dr. Harry W. Schaumburg (experienced counselor on sexual addictions / works with Christian leaders)

Out of the Shadows: Understanding Sexual Addiction, Third Edition, by Patrick J. Carnes, Ph.D. (speaker and clinical director of sexual disorders at The Meadows, Wickenburg, AZ)

Pure Desire by Ted Roberts (a pastor that overcame addiction to pornography) and Jack Hayford

Sex, Lies, and Forgiveness: Couples Speaking Out on Healing from Sex Addiction by Burt and Jennifer Schneider (used only—no longer in print)

The Sexual Man by Dr. Archibald D. Hart (based of nationwide research / refutes myths surrounding male sexuality)

Secret of Eve: Understanding the Mystery of Female Sexuality by Dr. Archibald D. Hart (used only—no longer in print)

She has a Secret: Understanding Female Sexual Addiction by D. Weiss, Ph.D.

A Way of Escape: Freedom from Sexual Strongholds by Neil T. Anderson (president of Freedom in Christ ministries) and **Freedom from Addiction:** Breaking the Bondage of Addiction and Finding Freedom in Christ by Neil T. Anderson, Mike Quarles, Julia Quarles, and Terry Whalin

Counseling / support groups

You may need professional assistance or counseling for past or present sexual sins. There are many worthy organizations.

References

- The Pornography Epidemic: A Catholic Approach by Peter C. Kleponis, Ph.D. Available at http://shop.womenofgrace.com/product/1340/books
- Be a Man by Fr. Larry Richards
- Boys to Men by Tim Gray and Curtis Martin
- Breaking Free: 12 Steps to Sexual Purity by Stephen Wood
- Contrary to Love: Helping the Sexual Addict by Patrick Carnes

- Every Man's Battle, Every Young Man's Battle, and Preparing your Son for Every Man's Battle by Stephen Arterburn and Fred Stoeker
- Healing the Wounds of Sexual Addiction by Mark R. Laaser
- In the Shadows of the Net by Patrick Carnes

- Out of the Shadows by Patrick Carnes
- Pure Eyes by Craig Gross and Steven Luff
- Shattered Vows by Debra Laaser
- The Pornography Trap by Ralph H. Earle, Jr. and Mark R. Laaser
- Theology of the Body for Beginners by Christopher West
- Wired for Intimacy: How Pornography Hijacks the Male Brain by William M. Struthers
- Your Sexually Addicted Spouse by B. Steffens and M. Means

Online Resources & References

- www.maritalhealing.com: The official website of The Institute for Marital Healing
- www.sexhelp.com: A site for those struggling with pornography use/addiction
- www.catholicmodesty.com: A site promoting modesty in dress
- www.familylifecenter.net: The official website for Family Live Center

International

- www.dads.org: The official website for St. Joseph's Covenant Keepers
- www.fathersforgood.com: A parenting website sponsored by the

  Knights of Columbus

- www.pornnomore.com: A Catholic website information, prayers and

  witness talks for those struggling with pornography

- www.settingcaptivesfree.com: A Christian website addressing a

  number of addictions, including pornography

- www.isafe.org: A website for internet safety education
- www.filterreview.com: A website that describes and rates different

  internet filters

- www.covenanteyes.com: An accountability service for those struggling with internet pornography. Use promo code: pursuitofholiness for

first month free!

- www.safeeyes.com: A service that blocks questionable websites
- www.focusonthefamily.com: A website that provides Christian

    resources for parenting

- www.familysafemedia.com: A website that provides resources for

    protecting your family online

- www.newlifepartners.com: A support group for wives whose husbands

    are caught in the web of sexual addiction

- www.pureonline.com: An online sex and pornography addiction

    recovery resources site that utilizes online workshops

- www.nationalcoalition.org: A website for the National Coalition for the

  Protection of Children and Families

- www.freedomeveryday.org: A site sponsored by L.I.F.E. Ministries

  (Living In Freedom Everyday), a sexual addiction recovery ministry

- www.flrl.org/truefreedom.com: A website sponsored by the Archdiocese of New York that provides resources for overcoming pornography use
- www.awomanshealingjourney.com: Online resources, support groups, and coaching for women whose husbands are addicted to pornography.
- www.reclaimsexualhealth.com: An online educational program designed to help Catholics who are struggling with sexual addiction.

- Patrick Carnes, Out of the Shadows, (Minneapolis: CompCare, 1983), 160.

- Ibid., 27.
- Craig Nakken, The Addictive Personality (New York: Harper & Row, 1988), 24. [up]

Author: Bill Perkins , text excerpted from his book When Good Men Are Tempted

About The Presenter

RAY PATRICK

Was raised in a broken home, his parents split at the age of seven; he attended one of the worst schools in West London (Christopher Wren). He was arrested on two occasions had his first bout with jail in 1988.

The cycle did not stop with Ray as he too experienced the pain of divorce, addiction and Negative behavior.

Ray lived homeless on the streets of Los Angeles, sleeping on floors in his car with no money or food.

Education

In 1989 headed to University in Alabama (Oakwood University) where he did Undergraduate studies in Religion and then to San Jose, CA where he completed Post Graduate Certifications specializing in breaking addictions and drug & gang identification using Rational Emotive Therapy, (changing negative thinking into positive behavior using CBT). CACAPD

Pastoral Ministry

Ray has been the assistant pastor at the Oakwood University church Huntsville AL, senior pastor Ephesus SDA Church San Jose California, pastor for community development Bakersfield California, youth pastor beacon light SDA Church Oakland CA, Currently world wide Evangelist for the SDA Church & Chaplin at The Eden School.

Media Ministry

Ray Has tackled media while in Los Angeles he was host of the T.V show AdventConnex and several radio show. Today he runs a daily Worldwide gospel show on www.medianetgospel.com London. In Feburary 2014 Ray was the speaker for the First French Adventist T.V channel, AD7 TV (an ASI sponsored project).

Mentoring & Counseling

He spent the last twelve years dealing with drug abuse and gang violence among the youth in California; LA, San Francisco, Oakland, San Jose, East Palo Alto and Bakersfield and now London. Ray worked in schools, youth clubs, churches, prisons, cooperation's (like NHS, Hammersmith and Fulham

Council, White City Community Centre, and London Borough of Brent) and on the street; fighting the war against drugs and negative behaviour, like anger and rage turning them into positive behaviour.

Community Ministry

Ray has done some pioneer work in the area of Spiritual Warfare and the devils attack on the mind which led to his first book "Warzone the battle for the mind". He has worked alongside Rev. Jessie Jackson's Operation Push, Magic Johnson (former NBA star), Joey Porter & Windell Tyler (NFL super bowl winning stars) on stop the violence programs. He taught how to use the word of God, to combat drugs, gangs and other Anti-Social behaviours. Most recently consulted with London mayor Boris Johnson on the Gang & drug problem in London and was featured in the Evening Standard Newspaper The Largest evening paper in the UK.

Missions

Ray is the current CEO and Founder of, **"Ray of Hope 4U"** a charity organization helping and Mentoring those in need around the world. Building schools and assisting orphans etc. In Zimbabwe, Tanzania, Gambia, Kenya, South Africa, and Uganda.

Because of Ray's struggles with Pornography from an early age, he now travels around the World doing his self-developed seminars entitled Taken By Porn and Breaking Addiction.

Email Address: www.rayofhope4u.co.uk **and** www.theoasisprojectad.com

Contact: Visit me on facebook Ray A Patrick